Richard Pearce

Richard Pearce knows the tide. Working from Golden Eagle gig shed on Bryher, Richard has been surrounded by ocean his whole life. This tiny island of Scilly is bound by the sea, by huge skies and dark nights, the smell of salt and seaweed, seeping fog and damp drizzle; it is a far cry from mainland living. Each day, every day he takes up his brushes and gazes across Hell Bay. His ancestors have lived here for generations; his life entwined in the stories wrapped around these shores. A tale of crofters, wreckers, tatties, pilchards and a never ending sea of blue, this is an intimate glimpse of his remote island life.

richard pearce: the story of an island artist...

9am walk to work

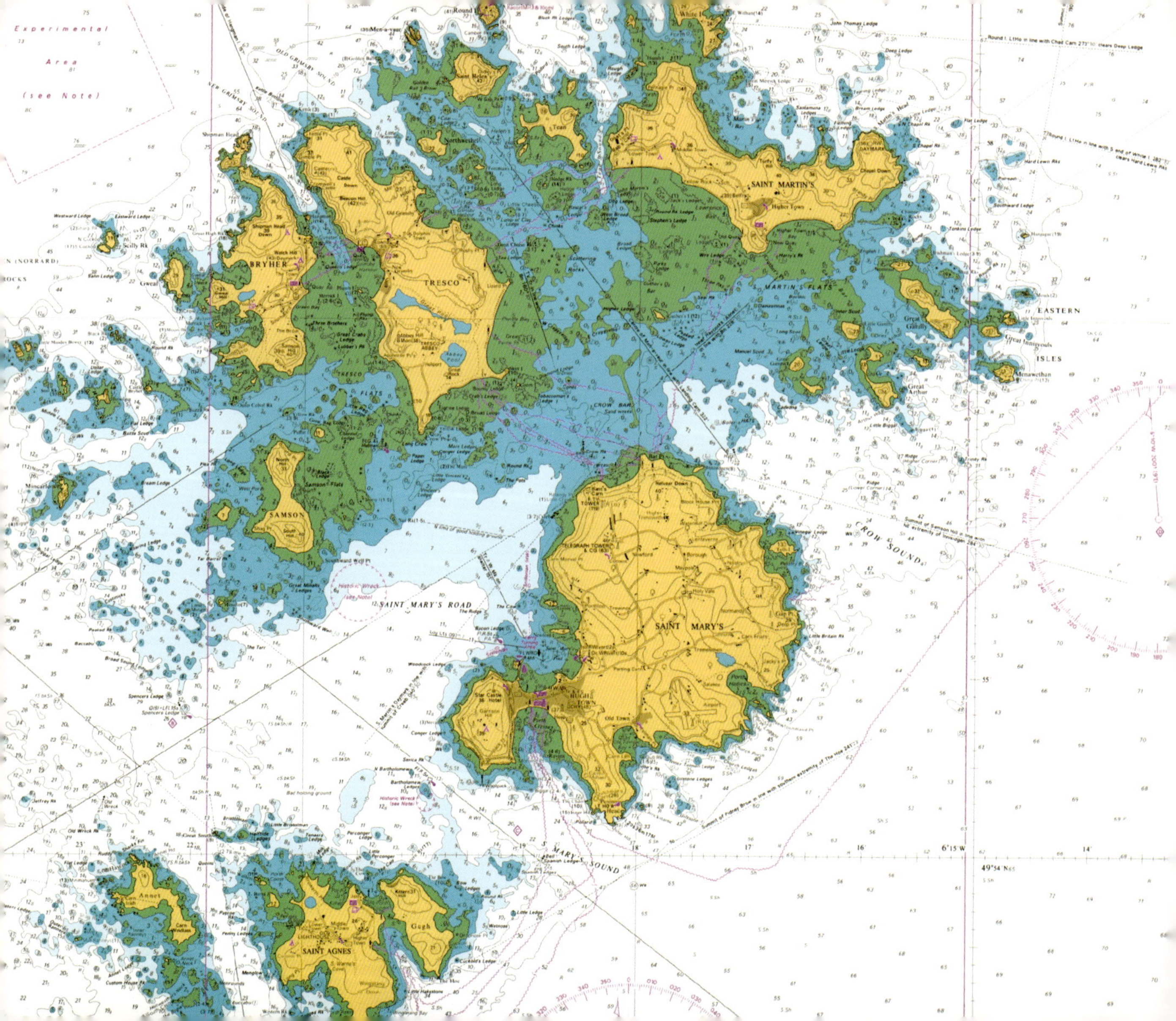

Experimental
Area
(see Note)
BRYHER
TRESCO
SAINT MARTIN'S
SAMSON
SAINT MARY'S
SAINT AGNES
Annet
Gugh
Tean
Saint Helens
Northwethel
Gweal
Scilly Rk
EASTERN
ISLES
Great Ganilly
Great Innisvouls
Menawethan
Great Arthur
TRESCO FLATS
ST MARTIN'S FLATS
CROW BAR
CROW SOUND
SAINT MARY'S ROAD
ST MARY'S SOUND
NEW GRIMSBY SOUND
OLD GRIMSBY SOUND
Samson Flats
Mincarlo
HUGH TOWN
Old Town
Star Castle
Historic Wreck (see Note)
6°15'W
49°54'N

isles of scilly...

inhabited... Saint Mary's, Saint Agnes, Tresco, Bryher, Saint Martins and Gugh. Gugh is the smallest with just three residents.

uninhabited... Samson, Annet, Malledgan, Tean, Northwethel, Saint Helen's, Round Island, Men-a-vaur, White Island, Eastern Isles, Gweal, Northern Rocks, Scilly Rock, Western Rocks, English Island, Zantman's Rock and Norrard Rocks are just some of more than 100 of the uninhabited islands.

left: © www.destinationsouthwest.co.uk

The crystal spine of Scilly; bathed in light, circled by shallows. The rhythm of the lighthouse beats through the pulse of the locals; many still remain who were born here. Over one hundred islands, only six of them occupied, lying just thirty miles off mainland Cornwall. So small are they that put them together and they can be crossed on a morning stroll. The landscape of this island cluster is as diverse as it is beautiful. From the Atlantic facing craggy tors to the fine strands of silver sand, the islands are an illustrious archipelago of flora, fauna, wildlife and real life. The human stories that thread this scattering of isles pitch and surge with the surrounding tides. With a legacy reaching back to the Stone Age, piracy, smuggling, ship building, fishing and farming have all graced these shores. Now reliant on tourism, out of the two thousand residents only thirty fishermen are still employed by the sea. No full time crofters remain. For Richard Pearce, he has been boy, crofter, father and artist on this land.

belonging...

I was born on St Mary's, the main island – it makes a difference. Island rivalry goes back generations. The Pearce's have lived on Scilly since 1830's. The Hicks family, on my Great Grandmother's side, go back forever. Growing up, sports day was big competition, the St Martin's boys out pegged us all – most were working the land by the time they were ten, we were soft in comparison. All the island children were taken by boat to Samson where we would race on the long spit of sand. Trestle tables were laid with sandwiches but mostly the wind got to them before we did. My father brought us up; four boys, two girls. Mother left on the day tripper, I was thirteen; I had a feeling she wasn't coming back. Dad was devastated. Some people were kind, others weren't; the freshly baked pasties our neighbour brought round were always good. I grew up and found my feet, travelling to places as far and vast as I ever imagined. It didn't last. The quiet shores of Scilly are home; they drew me back and the land of my ancestors will hold me forever.

left: Richard, aged 8, standing on the Garrison, St Mary's.

scillonian ancestors

off-islander…

As a boy I would stand on St Mary's strand and watch the flicker of the off-island lights. They seemed distant at night. Years later, when Caroline and I were married, we crossed that brief blue mile, leaving the main island for Bryher - the smallest of the inhabited off-islands. The distance was short but the change was immense. No mains electricity, no cars, little contact outside the borders of this tiny outcrop of land. On a small island everyone has their role. Johnny-Pots picks the crabs, Mike Pender is the fisherman, Ted is the blacksmith, builder and fireman, James and Neil are the boat men…I am the island artist. Living here took some getting used to. There are only 92 residents and in two hours you have walked the entire rim of the island. The beam of Bishop's Rock lighthouse lights my wall at night. It is like a heartbeat, a rhythm that reminds me of nights as a child, watching the sweep of the very same beam. We have lived on Bryher for twenty seven years and it is home yet somehow; you need to be born an off-islander to truly belong.

left: Bishop's Rock, Britain's tallest lighthouse.

I was a crofter before I was an artist. Our small-holding on Bryher had the biggest herd on the island – five cows and two pigs. We grew sols, daffs and tatties and days were spent ploughing, milking, picking and bunching. Our tea room served our own butter and clotted cream. The island didn't have mains electricity until 1985, everything ran off generators. Black smoke would pour from the freezer – it was something to do with the paraffin. Caroline would serve ice-cream with a permanently sooty face.

eeking an island living...

Later we moved to the old school teacher's house which we ran as a guest house. I would cook visitors my special spaghetti sauce... the more times I made it the more orange it became. I threw in anything I could find; I'm not sure what made it go so orange. We lived in the old generator shed at the back of the house, our daughter Helen was still a young child. Times were a lot harder but I feel a real nostalgia for that time, there was no television, no internet, no mobile phones and great socials at the community centre.

left: Daffodil pickers, St Mary's, Isles of Scilly.

false lights and wrecking...

The ocean surrounds us; we hear it, see it and smell it. It has fashioned the livelihoods of these islands for generations. Tales are told of piracy and wrecking, of false lights and looting. Notorious are the number of ships and lives lost off these shores. The shout of a ship gone down could bring everyone to the heart of the most mountainous sea. Lives were saved, goods were stowed – that was the Scillonian way. The wrecker's prayer says "Oh please Lord, let us pray for all on the sea. But if there's got to be wrecks, please send them to we." My grandfather claims that the first orange he ever saw came off a wreck and there are stories of Bryher men burying booty as big as grand pianos. They dug them up and learned to play as soon as customs went back to the mainland. When the Isabo went down in 1927, thirty two Italian sailors were saved. The men of Bryher launched the gig 'Czar' and rowed into the walls of the storm. I still have my great grandfather's medal, signed by Mussolini and awarded to all the islanders who saved those on board – it was the same ship that had been carrying the pianos. Not many boats are lost these days, but that doesn't mean there isn't still wrecking to be done – I regularly scout the beaches for a washed up hoard.

left: Waves crashing over Piper's Hole, Tresco, Isles of Scilly.

a sea change...

Some pit props got washed into the bay. Everyone was pulling what they could off the rocks. Good wrecking is like a good jumble sale except the only good thing I wrecked was my back. What followed were long days looking at the ceiling. That was fifteen years ago, it was when I started painting and I haven't stopped. My first exhibition was at the local community centre. Paintings sold - I was astonished. The ocean has long occupied my family, I may not struggle with it as much as my ancestors but I battle all the same - trying to find endless ways of coaxing the nature of the sea onto canvas.

right: Richard standing outside Golden Eagle studio.

support our
volunteer crews

art and the islands...

The relationship between art and the Scilly Isles goes back generations. Augustus Smith (1804 - 1872) arrived on the windswept, barren island of Tresco as Lord Proprietor in 1834. He was a knowledgeable plantsman and collector, creating the world renowned Tresco Abbey Gardens. Augustus had five great nieces; all talented painters and plantswomen who traced the daily lives of these islands in paint. Life continued to be recorded in this way for many generations, right up until the present day. As the current owners of Tresco, Robert and I have continued to encourage the relationship between artists and the islands. We began by opening a gallery in the little harbour of New Grimsby - Gallery Tresco. Our relationship with Richard began when he was asked to show his paintings at the gallery in 1991 and he has been exhibiting there ever since. The connection was reinforced with the opening of Hell Bay Hotel on Bryher when we commissioned a series of murals. His resulting vistas of aqua sea sliced by pure shards of sand remind me why Richard is such an enduring artist of these shores. The endless sweep of his paintings plays on the distant horizon, evoking the captivating space surrounding this small crop of land.

We are now lucky enough to own many of Richard's works and he and his family have become great friends over the years. The calm and restful quality of his paintings is testimony to the time he spends studying the sea and for us - we shall hope he continues to capture the atmosphere of the islands in his wonderful paintings for us to hang on our walls and enjoy forever.

Lucy Dorrien-Smith

the lifeline…

We wait for the launch; the launch comes with the tide. It brings our supplies from the mainland. A big delivery can interrupt everyone's day, especially if it's a horse or a tractor. I plan what I need well in advance – paints, canvases, frames – they all come on the ship. You get used to things not turning up or getting left on the quay – it's a way of life. Another way we are governed by the sea.

left: Unloading the 'Lyonesse Lady' on Bryher quay.

tides and trippers...

We are the only island to lose water. Our tide runs so low we can't take landings. No landings – no trippers. Caroline takes advantage of those days and drives across the channel to deliver paintings to Gallery Tresco. About six tides a year are low enough for her to make the trip, it's quite an occasion. I time the arrival of trippers by the tide. If it's low they get dropped off at Rushy Bay. By the time they have walked along the bay, looked for cowries, had an ice-cream, they generally reach the studio just before lunch. If it's high the boat drops them at the quay and they pass the studio early afternoon. In this way the tide effects how I plan my day. Visitors are disappointed if I'm not at the studio. Some come back every year to say hello. Many greet me like an old friend which I suppose I am.

right: Boarding 'Sea King' on Bryher quay.

SEA KING

TUDIO

golden eagle studio...

The studio was used from the mid 1800's to house the gig Golden Eagle and it most likely housed earlier gigs before then. It lay in a state of disrepair for many years until we went to the Duchy of Cornwall with a plan to dig it out of the sand dunes and convert it to a artist studio. We had to rebuild some of the walls and put a roof on; fortunately for us, whilst we were in the planning stages a hoard of timbers were washed ashore that were perfect for the roof. The studio opened in 1993. The sea will come in one day...

left: Richard outside Golden Eagle studio.

claustrophobia...

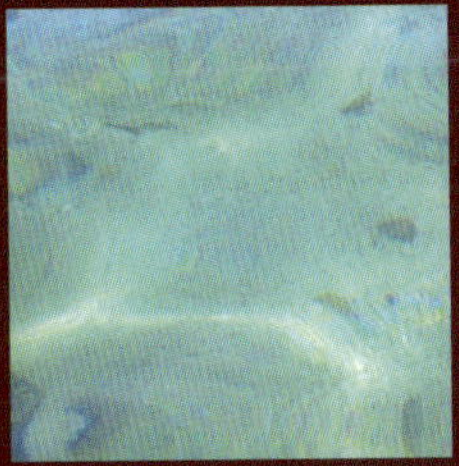

Everything gets washed up or found out on a small island – there are no secrets here. I get panic attacks. They generally start in small spaces. I'm not sure if that's because Scilly makes me feel free or confined - possibly both.

mrs p's generator...

Johnny-Pots and Billy decided to get their mum wired up to electricity. They bought the biggest generator, one that would do both houses, but she wasn't having any of it. "You can't trust electricity..." she'd say. When mains power arrived in 1985 she couldn't avoid it. Someone gave her a radio alarm clock but she would unplug it every night. When we were growing daff's Mrs P and Johnny would come over to help with the bunching. Caroline and Mrs P would have a sherry and me and Johnny would knock back his homemade beer.

scads and tatties all week, conga pie on sundays...

Some things don't change. Winkle picking on Good Friday and Lancing at full moon are old Scillonian customs. The lance are little fish that bury under the surface of the sand, revealed only in the moonlight by their shining silver bellies. At low water they can be raked into buckets for a fine supper. On a Spring tide Johnny-Pots can be seen down on the flats between Tresco and Bryher with his sprat nets. As the tide comes in his nets fill with fish. Scads, sprats and lance are fish found around these shores.

right: Spreading the nets, St Mary's, Isles of Scilly.

We are surrounded by vast reaches of indigo, cobalt, cerulean, turquoise, deepest marine, palest sapphire ...endless blue. I do paint the grey days. People don't like them so much. Three o'clock is when the light shifts. The back of the studio is floor to ceiling glass so I can watch the day as it moves through changes of colour. By honing everything down to the most minimal, a painting takes on its own life. I love the sand bar, a simple stark shard of sand striking through the shallows – it's enough. I walk from home to the studio every day – it takes a minute across the beach. It is different each time. A computer screen was washed up one day that held a huge fish. It must have swum in as a tiddler and kept on growing. I pondered the size of both our ponds.

When I started painting people wondered what I was doing looking out to sea all day. I was just taking it all in...sitting, listening, watching.

inspiration...

5pm back home

biography...

A self taught artist, Richard's paintings have been exhibited worldwide. But it is the delight visitors find when discovering him working against the backdrop of the Scilly Isles that gives his work such enduring appeal.

Solo Exhibitions
Camborne School of Mines, Cornwall
Bendigo Regional Arts Centre, Australia
Great Atlantic Mapworks, St Just, Cornwall

Mixed Exhibitions
Gallery Tresco, Isles of Scilly
Harbour Gallery, St Mary's, Isles of Scilly
University of Exeter
Manyung Gallery, Mt. Eliza, Victoria, Australia
Ecliptic Gallery, Armadale, Victoria, Australia
Lighthouse Gallery, Penzance, Cornwall
Webbs Road Fine Art, London
Bell Fine Art, Winchester, Hampshire
CUBE^3 Gallery, Plymouth
Contemporary Art Holdings, Cirencester

Publications
Selected Contemporary Artists of Australia by Michael Berry
A Royal Duchy by David Burnett and Peyto Slatter
Island Dreams by Great Atlantic Publications
Country Living Magazine

Richard's paintings have been published by IKEA, Waterstones and The Art Group.

right: The School House, Great Bay, Bryher, Isles of Scilly, 1987.

acknowledgements…

With thanks to Robert and Lucy Dorrien-Smith, Bryher Boats and the Tresco Heliport team for all their help shipping paintings, Gallery Tresco, Euan Rodgers, Philip Callan and staff at the Hellbay Hotel, Henry the Harbour Master, Chloë Wild, bodesign.co.uk, Johnny (for the sprats), Bryher islanders for their support, and every one of the lovely visitors who takes the time to come and see me in Golden Eagle Studio.

All paintings reproduced in 'depending on the tide' are by Richard Pearce.

Produced and written by Chloë Wild

Design by Bo Design

Photography by Kay Banfield, Phill Deason, Francis Hosken, Vicki Smith and Jill Wilson.

Published by Caroline Soundy 2007

ISBN 978 0 9555602 0 0